Persuasion Superpowers
X-Ray Body Reading

Tap the power to virtually

see into other

people's

minds

✖

By BBlackwood

ISBN: 978-0-6151-6974-3

DISCLAIMER AND TERMS OF USE AGREEMENT

The author and publisher have used their best efforts in preparing this report, but make no representation or warranties with respect to the accuracy, applicability, fitness or completeness of the contents of this report. The information contained in this report is strictly for educational purposes. Therefore, if you apply ideas contained in this report, you are taking full responsibility for your actions.

Your level of improvement in attaining the results claimed in our materials depends on the time you devote to the program, ideas and techniques mentioned, knowledge and various skills. Since these factors differ according to individuals, we cannot guarantee your success or improvement level. Nor are we responsible for any of your actions.

The author and publisher disclaim any warranties (express or implied), merchantability or fitness for any particular purpose. The author and publisher shall in no event be held liable to any party for any direct, indirect, punitive, special, incidental or other consequential damages arising directly or indirectly from any use of this material, which is provided "as is" and without warranties.

As always, the advice of a competent professional should be sought.

The author and publisher do not warrant the performance, effectiveness or applicability of any sites listed or linked to in this report. All links are for information purposes only and are not warranted for content, accuracy or any other implied or explicit purpose.

TABLE OF CONTENTS

"Up, up and away!"

– Superman

Have you ever looked at a superhero character in comic books, graphic novels or on film and thought to yourself: *" I need a secret superpower"*? Many people have wished that, haven't they? They've said to themselves: "If I could bend steel bars or see through rock or turn time backwards, think of the things I could accomplish!"

I'm BBlackwood and I've certainly felt like that. As a youth, I can't tell you how many chairs, bookcases and finally garage roofs I jumped off, wearing my mother's best bath towel as a cape, in an attempt to take to the air like my Saturday morning TV hero....

Look! Up in the sky! It's a bird, it's a plane – it's... oof!

Luckily, I never broke any bones. I never flew, either. I'm pretty hardheaded, though; I didn't give up. For most of my lifetime, I've searched for ways to develop unique powers –

superpowers that would allow me to achieve things others only dreamed about.

That sounds crazy, right? *Superpowers?*

Fact is, I found The Way. (Short for what I call The Way to Get Your Way.)

And you know the real *secret* to these secret superpowers? Like a student at Dr. Xavier's Academy, you have the capabilities within you right *now* – in fact, you are probably using some of these special resources every day without realizing their full potential. All most people need to ramp these skills up to superpower level is to refine them and practice them.

If you study, learn and truly apply the secrets I'm going to share with you through this guide, you *will* have powers to accomplish things others only dream about.

How would you like to be able to immediately start **bonding with anyone you choose** and to create deep rapport within minutes?

What if you could **virtually *see* into other people's**

minds – as if with X-Ray Vision – and could tell things they're thinking that perhaps *they* don't even consciously know?

Imagine if you could quickly sense people's hotbuttons, dislikes, fears, needs and wants – wouldn't that give you incredible strength to use in persuading them to your way?

X-Ray Body Reading gives me those persuasion powers; now you can use those skills to get your way, too.

I call that super. I think you will call it super, too.

Says Who?

I'm not a psychologist or behavioral scientist. I'm a career persuader – in advertising, public relations and, sometimes politics. Through a 35-year career (so far), if I didn't persuade, I didn't get paid. So, theories, postulations, possibilities – I find all that fascinating but as a hobby.

To feed my family, I had to find persuasion methods that worked – not in theory, or in one university study, but out in the real world with real people. And the methods had to be successful 80, 90, 100% of the time.

I needed to become *Supersuader!*

So, I mined mountains of material, read Amazon rivers of books and sought out articles, tapes, videos, CDs, interviews and more. For over three decades, I have studied, tested, refined, discarded and retested. I've plundered the most powerful knowledge on the subject from the fields of human relations, psychology, hypnosis, neurolinguistic programming, stage mindreading, kinesics, proximics and a world of other topics both mundane and ethereal. Over years, I have distilled it all down to the vital essence – that famous 20% that yields 80% of all positive results.

In simplest terms, the stuff that *works*.

So, are you ready to fly?

Let's go jump off some roofs!

(The Super Secret)

Every hero and heroine have some source for their special powers, whether it's the bite of a mutated spider, a magic amulet or a convenient industrial accident. This is the power behind the superpower.

So, what is the source of the persuasion superpowers we're going to develop? Are you ready? Here is the most powerful super secret you will learn from me:

TRUST.

It's so simple, yet so incredibly powerful. Condensed down to the most essential and elegant explanation of everything I've learned about persuasion (aka Getting Your Way) in 35 years of study – TRUST.

The power of TRUST is so potent that once you master the ability to develop it, you will be able to do more with it than you may have dreamed possible.

That may sound incredibly naïve and simplistic to you but consider what the word really means. My dictionary defines the word TRUST as "firm belief in the reliability, truth, ability or strength of someone or something."

The secondary meaning given is "acceptance of the truth of a statement without evidence or investigation." As in: "He took what she said on TRUST."

Think about it for a moment. If you were totally TRUSTed, what could you achieve? If people have a *firm belief* in your *reliability*, your *truth*, your *ability*, your *strength*, what would they do for you?

Answer: **Anything.**

People who TRUST you will give you their friendship, will give you their love, will give you their money. In fact, if you're *really* TRUSTed, people will give you whatever you want.

A simple truth. But not necessarily simple to achieve.

The world can often seem a huge, jostling, hard-knock place. It's full of dangers, unseen pitfalls and fears, both real and imagined. TRUST is often in short supply; disTRUST sometimes seems a much more realistic answer.

Exactly. That's part of the power of TRUST – scarcity.

TRUST *can* still be created, however. In fact, most of us deeply long to TRUST and to be justified in TRUSTing. (Another vital component of TRUST-Power.)

I have searched out the best knowledge about how to build TRUST and how to use it *ethically* in the most positive ways. I've spent years condensing it down to its most vital essence for myself, and now for you.

What you're reading now will show you tested ways to start building TRUST instantly with almost anyone, so you can get what you need in life again and again – while giving the other person what he or she needs.

(And, yes, repeating the word TRUST over and over in capital letters is a persuasion technique – a form of hypnotic writing. I'm obviously not being covert about it; I'm using it here to keep reminding you: TRUST is the source of all persuasion superpowers.)

❎ A Few Words About Nouns

Let's make it easier on all of us. Instead of using "the person you are trying to persuade" through this book, I will simply refer to that other person in the persuasion process as *Your Partner*. If there is more than one, I'll write Your Partners.

The classic terminology of advertising and marketing often casts "the person you are trying to persuade" in terms not of positive influence but of war: target. When being less aggressive, advertisers usually type "the person" as something passive and inert (audience) or merely a statistic (demographic).

If the potent power that will make us truly persuasive is TRUST, doesn't it make sense to think of the other person in the process not as an enemy or faceless cipher but as a human being worthy of respect? (You certainly will *not* build TRUST if you treat people like anything less.)

Persuasion is a two-way enterprise, an exchange back and forth. In fact, in many ways it's like a dance, with you as the lead and the other person responding to your gentle but expert guidance. That other person in the dance is Your Partner.

Sometimes Your Partner will be male, sometimes female. So, to make it even easier, I will often refer to Your Partner as just *he* or *she*.

"Go, X-Ray Boy!"

– Megaton Man

You may have heard that only 3% of all one-to-one communication is actual verbal language. The rest is what is classed as paralinguistics: body language, involuntary eye movement, micro-expression and non-verbal sounds.

That popular "fact" is an overstatement, a misinterpretation of some findings by psychology researcher Albert Mehrabian. But even the most conservative theorists think that at least half of our one-to-one communication takes place in a non-verbal way and most likely it's in the 60-75% range.

So, like an iceberg, **as much as 3/4 of our communication is below the surface.** There are our words up at the top and then there is much more we're saying hidden deep *below* the surface of our spoken words.

X-Ray Body Reading gives you the power to see below that surface and read those hidden communications, to actually know what someone is thinking and feeling, no matter what she says. It really is like having a sort of X-Ray Vision into people's *minds*.

Does that sound too fantastic to believe?

I have made a serious study of people who are attributed with the power to read minds. So far, I have met no one with positive proof of ESP. But I know for a fact that *you* can read *thoughts* – and you do so every day.

Try it out: You see a man and woman in their 30s, arm in arm, strolling down the sidewalk in a pleasant suburban neighborhood. He has a big grin on his face; she has not. A buff 19-year-old jock jogs by, shirt off, looking golden in the afternoon sun. The woman turns her eyes very casually as the jock passes. The boy catches her look, throws her a crooked smile and, almost an afterthought, blows her a kiss. Now her head turns to watch the jogger until he's well up the street, and even then there's a trace of his crooked smile on her lips. When she turns back, she finds that her escort has stopped and is frowning at her, his hands on his hips, his chest inflated. His bottom lip sticks out. She rolls her eyes and heaves a tiny sigh.

I'll bet you could tell me every thought that crossed both those people's minds (and maybe the jogger's).

Try it again. Look at the young woman on the next page.

⊠ What Is She Thinking?

(Hint: It's Not Good)

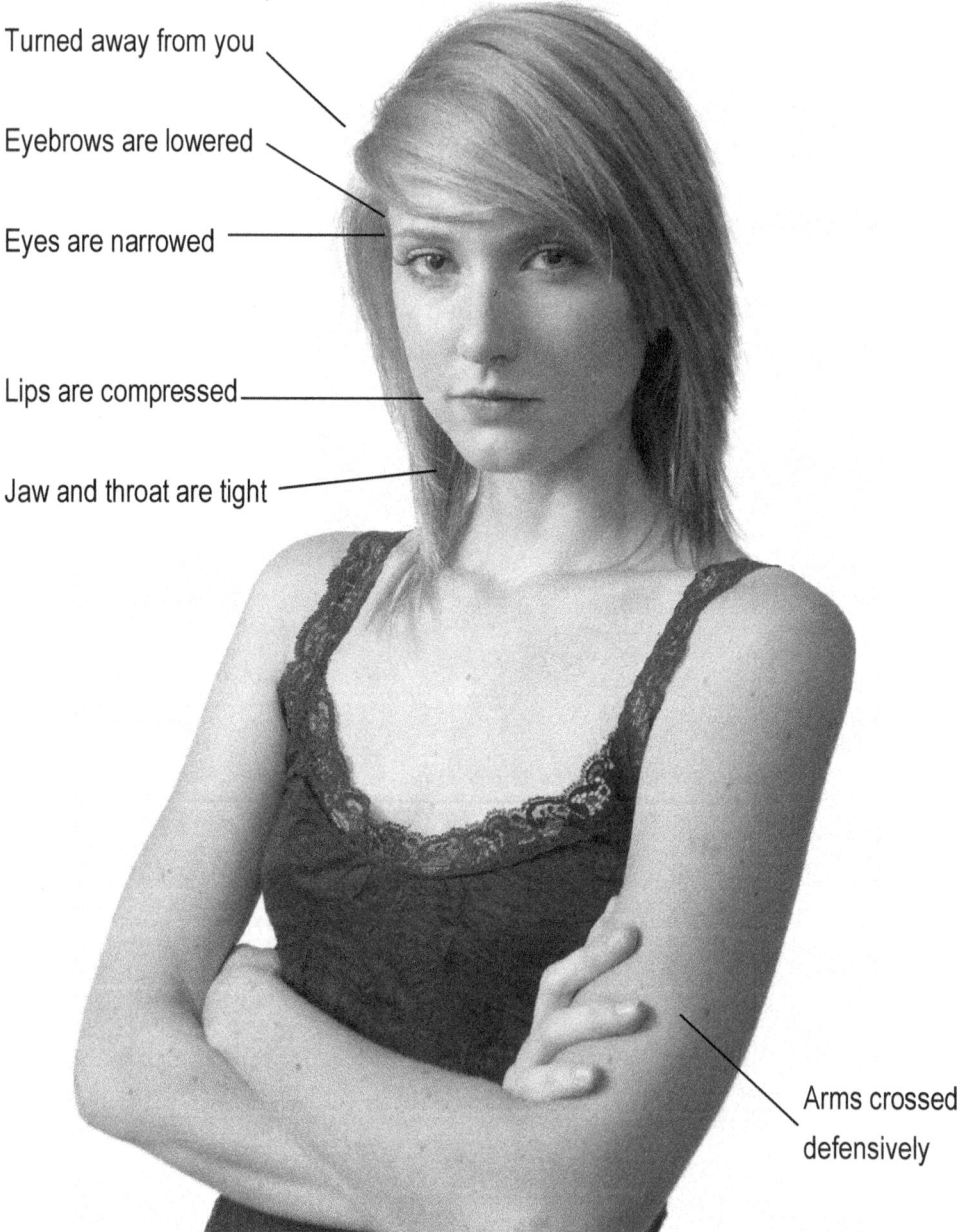

Turned away from you

Eyebrows are lowered

Eyes are narrowed

Lips are compressed

Jaw and throat are tight

Arms crossed
defensively

See, you *can* read thoughts – by reading body language.

I'm going to show you how to ramp up that power of body reading and focus it like X-Ray Vision to help you get what you want and need.

But I'm assuming you're busy – you have plenty on your plate without having to learn an entire system of complex body, eye and sound cues. There are $300, 12-CD sets just teaching body reading. And they're wonderful. But I'm going to share with you the vital 20% of that knowledge that will help you the most.

If you want to persuade people, if you want to get your way, here are the two crucial phases of this knowledge:

1. *You need to know when you are winning over someone* to your point of view, to your proposal – to your way.

2. And *you need to know when you're losing ground* with Your Partner.

When you're persuading them. And when you're losing them. That is your radar and your guidance system. That tells you if you're on-track or if you need to shift tactics. In this guide, you will learn the most-used unconscious gestures and expressions that tell when Your Partner is feeling positive about you, when he is seriously considering your proposal and when he is ready to say "yes." You will also learn the signals that say Your Partner is not feeling positive about you, when you are losing her, and when to step back and start over. (Or run!)

You also need to know *when they're telling you the truth and *when they're lying.* For a variety of reasons we won't explore now, people will lie to you. How can you persuade anyone to your way of thinking unless you truly *know* how he or she is thinking? So, you must know when people are lying to you and when they are telling you the actual truth. You'll learn that crucial skill as well.

These skills will be of practical use to you in the most universal persuasion situations: business or governmental, romance, interaction with family or friend, and social exchange. Really, those situations account for almost all the persuasion needs I've been able to uncover.

Ready? Go, X-Ray Boy (and Girl)!

If Your Partner is interested in your offer...

1. Positive Facial Cues

Watch the eyes. Eyes and mouth, as you know, are usually people's most expressive features. If someone is interested in you and what you're proposing, they will give you *more and longer eye contact*.

(Unbreaking staring is a sign of hostility or dominance.)

Your Partner's eyes will be open and relaxed if he's interested. As he grows more interested, watch for signs of his eyes opening wider in appreciation. It's almost as if the more pleasing you are to the other person, the more that person wants of you in their eyes.

Dilated pupils are very good indicators. Even the best actor can't control pupil dilation and contraction. It is autonomic, controlled by the inner mind via the nerves. As such, it can be a very truthful indicator of interest. Again, it's almost as if he is opening up to let you in *visually*.

On the other side of the coin, Your Partner will respond to your eye-cues, including the size of your pupils. He will respond more positively to you if *your* eyes are open in interest and your pupils are large.

How can you control an uncontrollable nervous function?

TIP: By far the *surest* way to make your own body language persuasive is just to truly decide you like the person you're with and wish them to succeed and prosper. You'll not need to worry much about yourself after that – your true inner mind will guide your every move, leaving you to concentrate on reading the signals of Your Partner.

There will be more about this in the final section on your body language. For now, let's go back to the other positive signs you can read in Your Partner.

Smiles – the most universal sign of acceptance and appreciation. Even blind babies smile from birth. It is born into us, bred into us, and is also by far the most commonly faked expression cue.

A real smile has some kind of magic in it, doesn't it? Look at an old picture of you posing, maybe some group shot, trying to sell a smile as phony as dime store pearls. Now find one of you really having a great time, compare the smiles.

⊠ Signs of An Artificial Smile

Smile only affects his mouth – not the rest of his face

Brows, eyes, cheeks uninvolved

Smile pulls to his left
(Right-handed person)

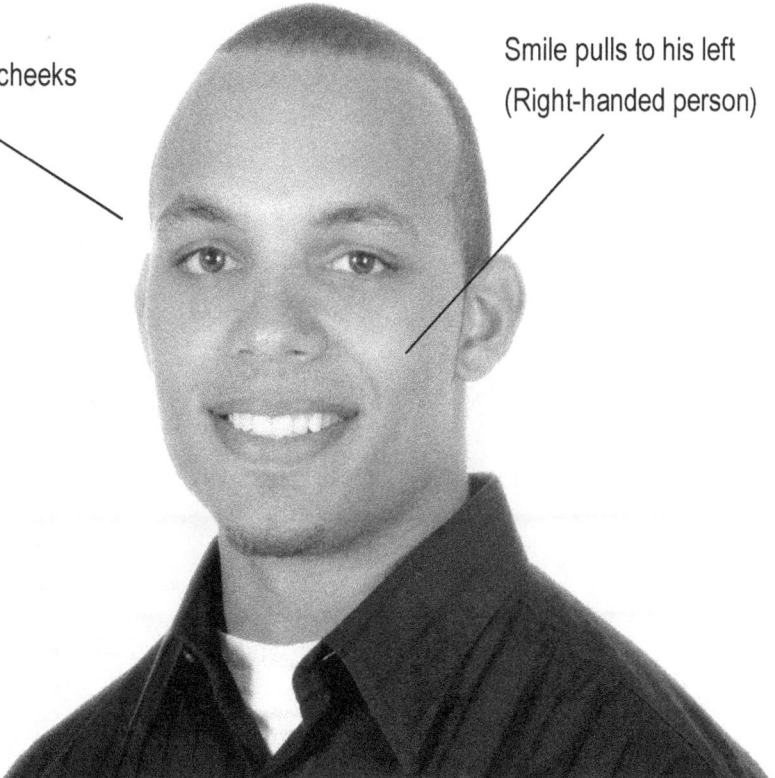

With smiles, or any expression really, watch the left side of the face – *their* left side. The left side of our bodies, faces included, tends to be controlled by the right side of the brain, and vice versa on the other side. To simplify it drastically, the right brain tends to reflect the emotional part of us, the *truthful* part of us, in the sense that we most often act from feelings rather than from thoughts.

So, a smile that pulls to the right could be giving an indication that it's real. But if the person is left-handed, be careful, that often reverses the "code." Unfortunately, not always.

Following the eyes and the smile, the eyebrows are third in expressive importance. The majority of the time, they reinforce and further define the message of the eyes. But when eyes and eyebrows present at odds with each other – then it gets interesting.

Simple rules for eyebrows:

• Up is generally good

• Way up into furrowed brow is *not* good – confusion and/or shock is not a very effective TRUST-builder

⊠ Positive Facial Cues

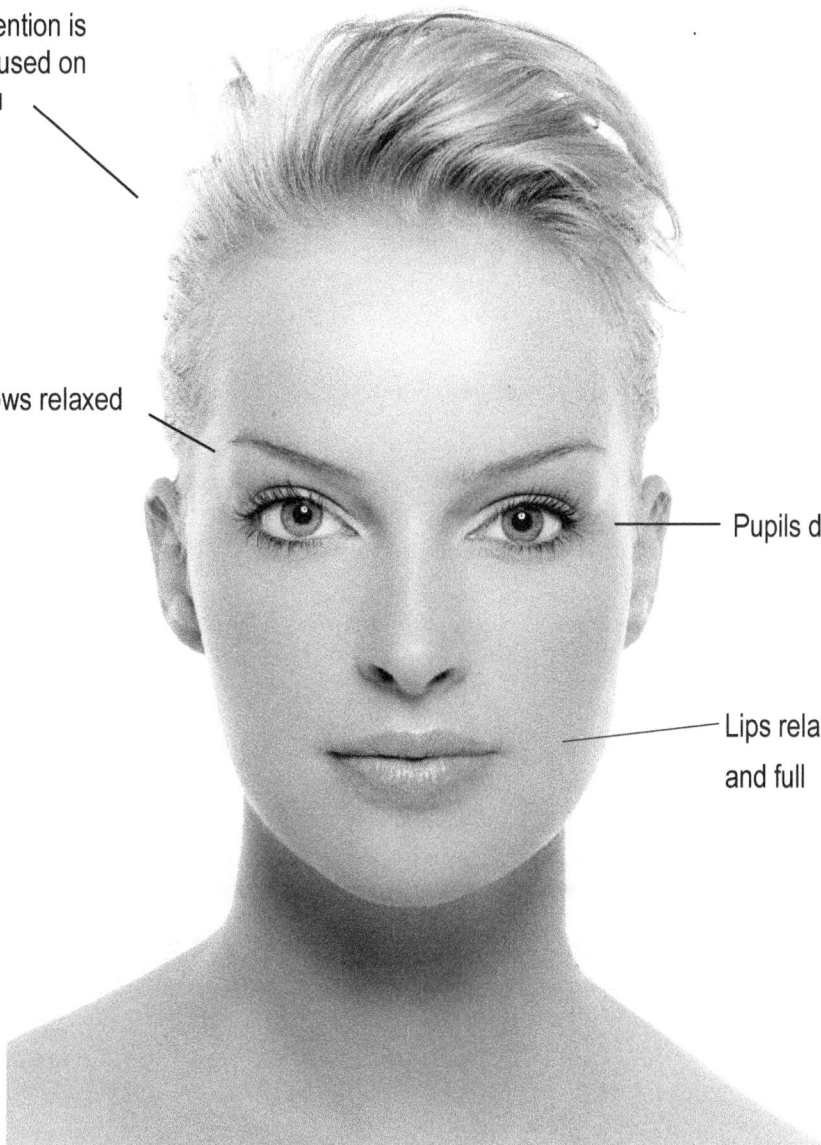

Attention is focused on you

Brows relaxed

Pupils dilated

Lips relaxed and full

2. Positive Cues of Head, Hands and Feet

If Your Partner's head is leaning toward you, that's a good sign. It's as if he's being pulled your way by his mind. The more he leans toward you, the... well, more he's *inclined* to go your way. (Sometimes the unconscious mind is remarkably literal.)

Nodding, of course, is a universal sign of agreement or encouragement, signaling, "yes, go on...." Nods require no great acting skill so they are not always sincere.

Consistent, well-timed nods do suggest that the prospect is at least paying attention. Single and double headnods are good signs; more could show he's just going through the motions.

So, what must *you* do to build TRUST? Show interest in Your Partner. You've already got your eyes open wide, right? Lean forward, pay attention and nod encouragingly.

Hands, of course, seem just made for expression and with many people, that's where cues will leak out. You want to see open-handed gestures, open palms, open-arm gestures. People who are open to you intellectually and emotionally often show it by being open physically.

But if you want to really know what a person is thinking, look to their *feet*. Even if Your Partner is adept at controlling and masking his body language, he probably is too distracted to worry about the body parts that are (literally) farthest from his mind.

Often Your Partner's feet will be pointed where her mind is really focused, whatever else the rest of her body is doing. This is so simple that you might pass over it. You shouldn't. In the old days, fortunetellers and séance artists could build lucrative careers out of just following the cues of their clients' feet.

⊠ Positive Body Stance

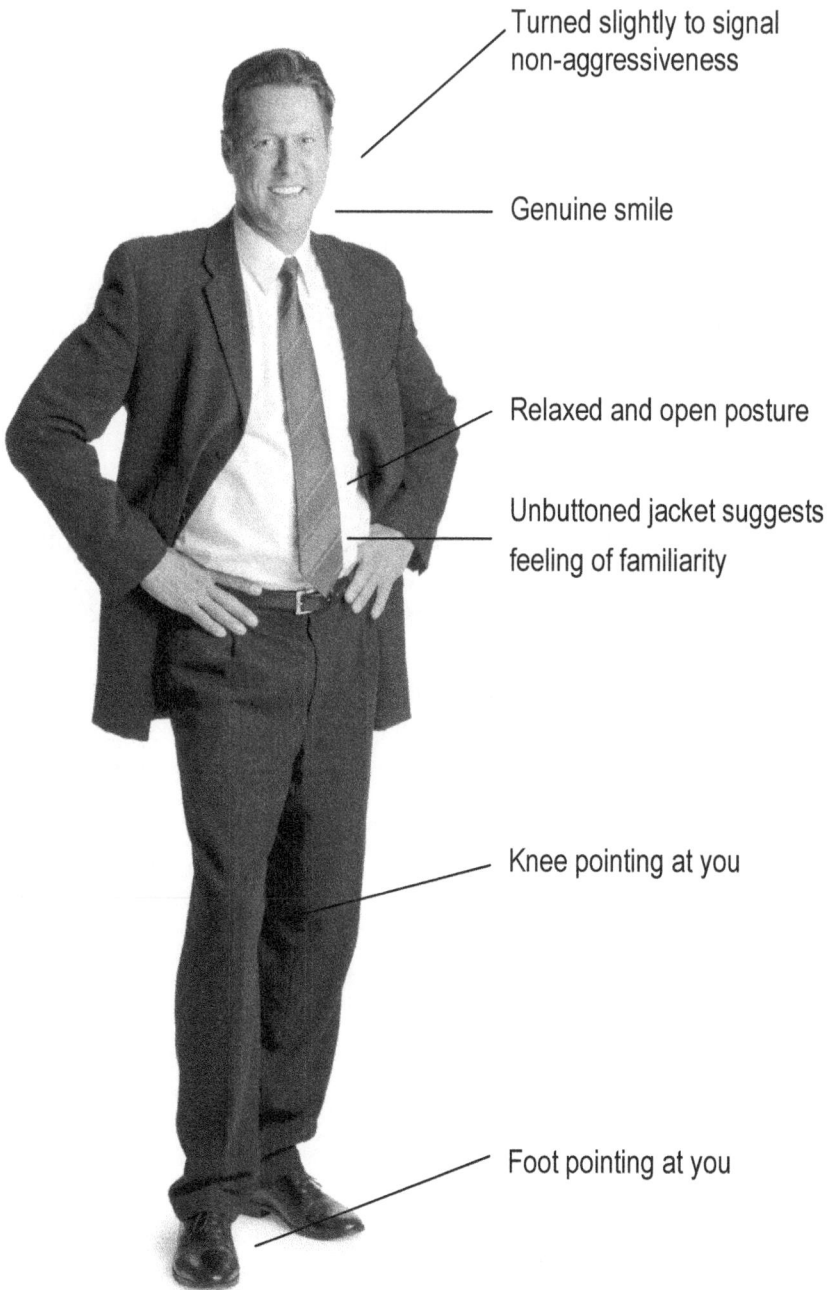

Turned slightly to signal non-aggressiveness

Genuine smile

Relaxed and open posture

Unbuttoned jacket suggests feeling of familiarity

Knee pointing at you

Foot pointing at you

If Your Partner Is Accepting Your Proposal...

His hands are open, perhaps resting relaxed and flat on the table.

He may slightly loosen clothing – taking off a jacket, unbuttoning a collar or rolling up his sleeves. This indicates that he now has feelings of acceptance and collaboration.

She will show attention to what you are saying and doing. She will follow you with her eyes, her head.

She may stroke her chin while considering, or fiddle with her glasses, cleaning them or chewing on the earpiece. People who do this may be hesitating because they need more details, or they may just be buying thinking time.

Chin resting in palm can be a good sign, indicating that he's open to hearing more about what you have to say. The more the head is supported by the hand, though, the more bored he is becoming with what you're saying.

☒ Positive Facial Cues: Acceptance

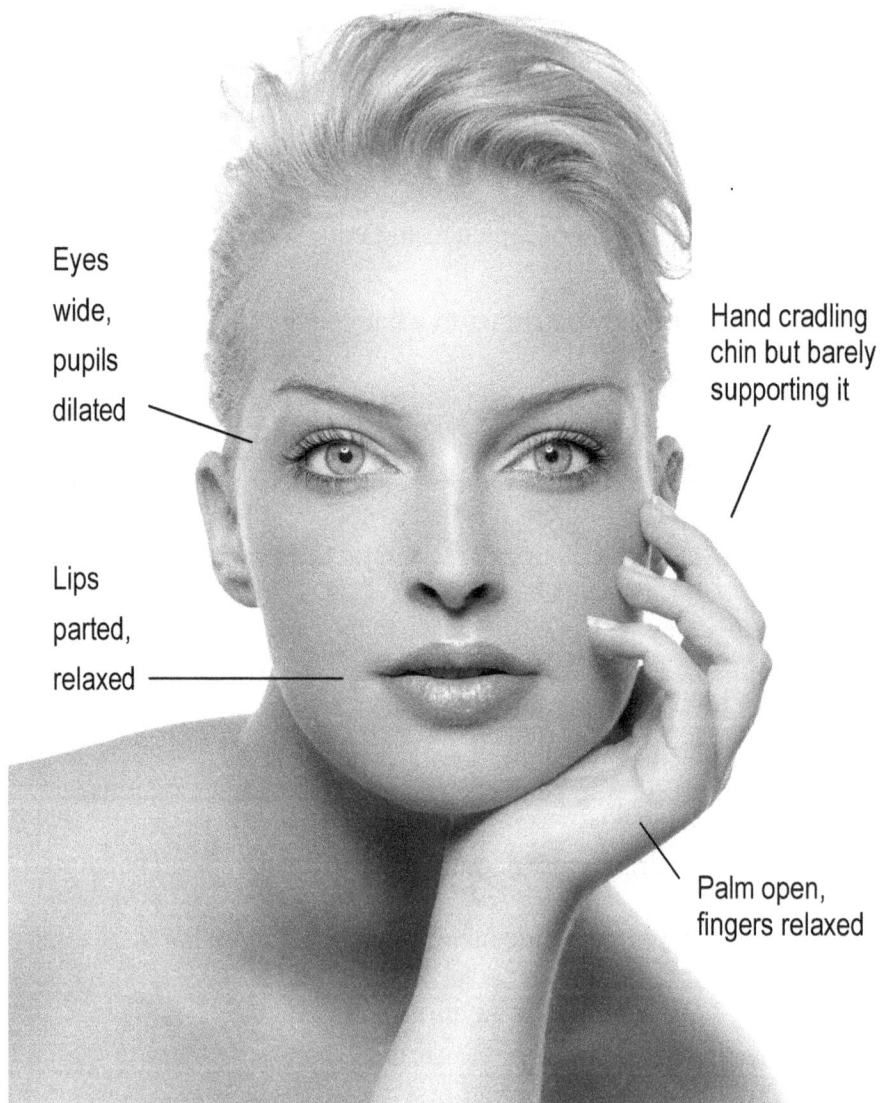

Eyes wide, pupils dilated

Hand cradling chin but barely supporting it

Lips parted, relaxed

Palm open, fingers relaxed

When Your Partner Is About To Commit...

When Your Partner is almost convinced, he may become slightly agitated and squirm a bit, a last flush of resistance against committing to you.

He is thinking about all the consequences of saying "yes," trying to spot a problem that might result. This is the time to gently but firmly recap the things you've said to bring him to this point, reminding him of the positives.

Here are some signs that your prospect has decided to move forward. In the sales world, these are known as *buying signals*.

After the last-minute worry has passed, her expression may lighten, she may grin, maybe impishly or even ruefully, as if saying, "I hope I don't regret this..." Her eyes and pupils may widen. She breathes deeper, and holds the breath longer. She licks her lips in anticipation. If she doesn't actually lick them, her lips may swell slightly as the tension in her mouth is relaxed.

She has made the leap – a psychological commitment –
now she is eager to act, excited and a little keyed-up.

That, friends, is the time to seal the deal.

If Your Partner Is *Dis*interested...

Closed fists are universal signs of something hidden or readiness to fight – very negative cues in body language.

Probably the bit of body language wisdom that most people know best is that crossed arms are a sign of wariness or disbelief. Any closed body posture, from tightly crossed legs to hunched shoulders, suggests negative energy. The prospect is literally building a barrier between you.

Sometimes Your Partner will actually create a physical barrier by putting her glasses or a pen or some other inanimate object on a table between you – or sometimes in her hand held in front of her – as a sort of symbolic blockade against you. Either you're saying the wrong thing, or you're moving too fast in your proposal. You need to slow down and go back to building TRUST if this happens.

If Your Partner grabs or pulls on his ear, it can demonstrate anxiousness. Often it is a sign that he has heard enough – or wants to speak up himself.

Scratching the neck, especially if using the index finger of the dominant hand, shows you've just said something that the listener disagrees with or doubts. He's saying, "Hmmm. I don't know…."

An oblong smile is a courtesy smile. The lips are pulled back from the teeth all around, forming an oblong grimace that is a fake smile. Real smiles affect the whole face – cheeks, eyes, eyebrows, nose – fake smiles barely make it past the mouth.

If Your Partner takes care of a small personal task, say removing a piece of jewelry or rolling up her sleeves, while she still pays attention to you, it suggests that she is comfortable with you. You're building TRUST.

Be careful, though, when Your Partner takes care of very personal tasks – filing or clipping nails, picking or flossing teeth and so on. That shows *disdain.*

Interrupting you, changing the subject being discussed and attending to other business, such as phone calls or emails, are major signs that you've lost him. You need to start again and quickly build a bridge of TRUST between you.

But first, you've got to get his attention back. A question, preferably combined with leaning in toward the person, will usually bring his attention back to you. If that doesn't work, make a sweeping gesture with your hand as you talk – that should draw his eye.

I carry a silver writing pen with me. When I gesture with that, not only is there movement, but a flash of reflected light.

That pen is my secret weapon, the pride of my batbelt. I'll show you the really cool things you can do with a simple pen in later guides. (It has to do with using covert hypnotic persuasion.)

⊠ Negative Facial Cues: Irritation/Disbelief

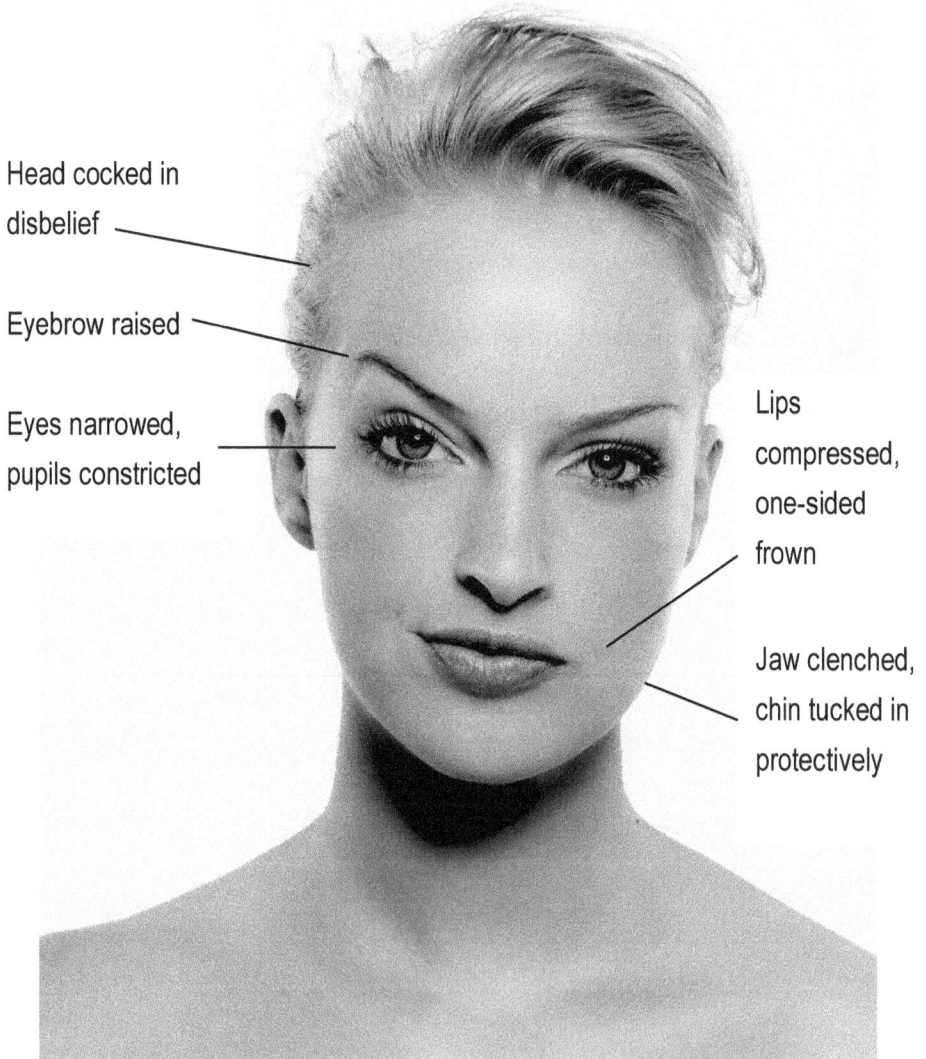

Head cocked in
disbelief

Eyebrow raised

Eyes narrowed,
pupils constricted

Lips
compressed,
one-sided
frown

Jaw clenched,
chin tucked in
protectively

If Your Partner Is Lying…

This is important for all of us – how to become Human Lie Detectors. There are whole books written on this, but I'll give you my vital 20%.

Most people don't like to lie. Even if we think we don't mind, most of us hold a deeply ingrained idea that lying is wrong. And even more, most of us fear being exposed as a liar. The price of being caught lying in our society carries with it a whole list of painful consequences from loss of reputation to loss of freedom – as in incarceration for perjury.

So, when people *do* lie to us, they often unconsciously leak hints of the internal strain.

Remember I said that the unconscious mind can be very literal? Liars will often be compelled to try to hide or suppress the lie physically. As they lie, they will often mask their mouth in some way. It could be as small as a finger on the lip, as if they are trying to hold the lips together. Or they might unconsciously try to *contain* the lie by speaking behind their hand or into a fist.

Clinched lips, thinner, perhaps paler, suggest inner turmoil and perhaps physically preparing to lie. Watch for signals that the head is *locking down* – jaw tightened, mouth taut, teeth clinched.

You've heard the expression, "He lied through his teeth"? People often do; they clinch their teeth and move their mouth less when they lie. Again, their minds are literally trying to hold back the lie.

A visible tightening of the throat is another indication of trying to choke off the untruth. Dry mouth and increased swallowing may accompany this; a strangled or hoarse voice could be another symptom – and clue.

Even the nose gets involved in lying. Remember Pinocchio? Collodi's evergreen fable was based on smart observation all those years ago. There is an internal struggle when we lie, causing our blood pressure to rise in many cases.

Blood moving into the face engorges the nose and it actually *grows* a tiny bit, like Pinocchio's.

Increased pressure causes the nose to tingle. So, watch for touching, rubbing or scratching the nose – these can indicate deceit. Picking the nose… that's just bad manners.

The increased blood pressure from lying may cause the neck to swell also, causing that tugging-at-the-collar, "is it hot in here or is it just me" behavior lying people often exhibit – at least in old movies. Flushing with color, of course, also shows that some strong emotion is present.

In general, timing between gestures and words may just seem off, perhaps mechanical or overly controlled.

A falsely accused person will usually go on the *offensive*; a liar will go on the defensive.

Touching, pointing and strong gestures can often signal that Your Partner is truthful. Liars will not make gestures that are as strong or touch you as much as truth-tellers.

A liar will want you to believe him; a falsely accused person will want you to *understand* him.

Lies And Eyes

The eyes hold an almost mythic status in the lore of lying. Most liars believe that if they are caught lying, it will be because their eyes gave them away. This belief must stem partly from the poetic notion that the eyes are windows into the soul. Somewhere deep inside the liar, a whispered voice tells her that the black of her pupils will reveal the color of her lying soul, so she won't meet your gaze.

Shifty-eyed or just simply *shifty* are terms that have long been popular synonyms for liar – or at least for someone who is *likely* to lie to you. That's the origin of the BB-eyed villain of fiction, too – but is it really true?

Well, yes and no.

It is true, as with the mouth not wanting to let the lie out, not looking at you can be a strong sign that Your Partner is trying to distance himself from a lie. Just the fact that many people believe that eyes cannot lie often makes it a reality.

Rubbing the eye is another way of avoiding looking at you. Or it could be allergies, so don't let that be your only clue.

Looking intently at papers, the television, the passing traffic, whatever can be a sign that Your Partner is hiding his eyes from you.

Sunglasses, of course, have been assisting deceivers almost since the first person figured how to darken optical glass with smoke. Certainly, if Your Partner is wearing shades in an inappropriate way – at night, indoors, in a restaurant – and is not an Elvis impersonator, be alert for other signs.

☒ Negative Facial Cues: Lying

Face turned, refusal to meet your eyes

Eyes looking off. Is she inventing a response?

Blushing

Mouth slack as if hesitant to form lie

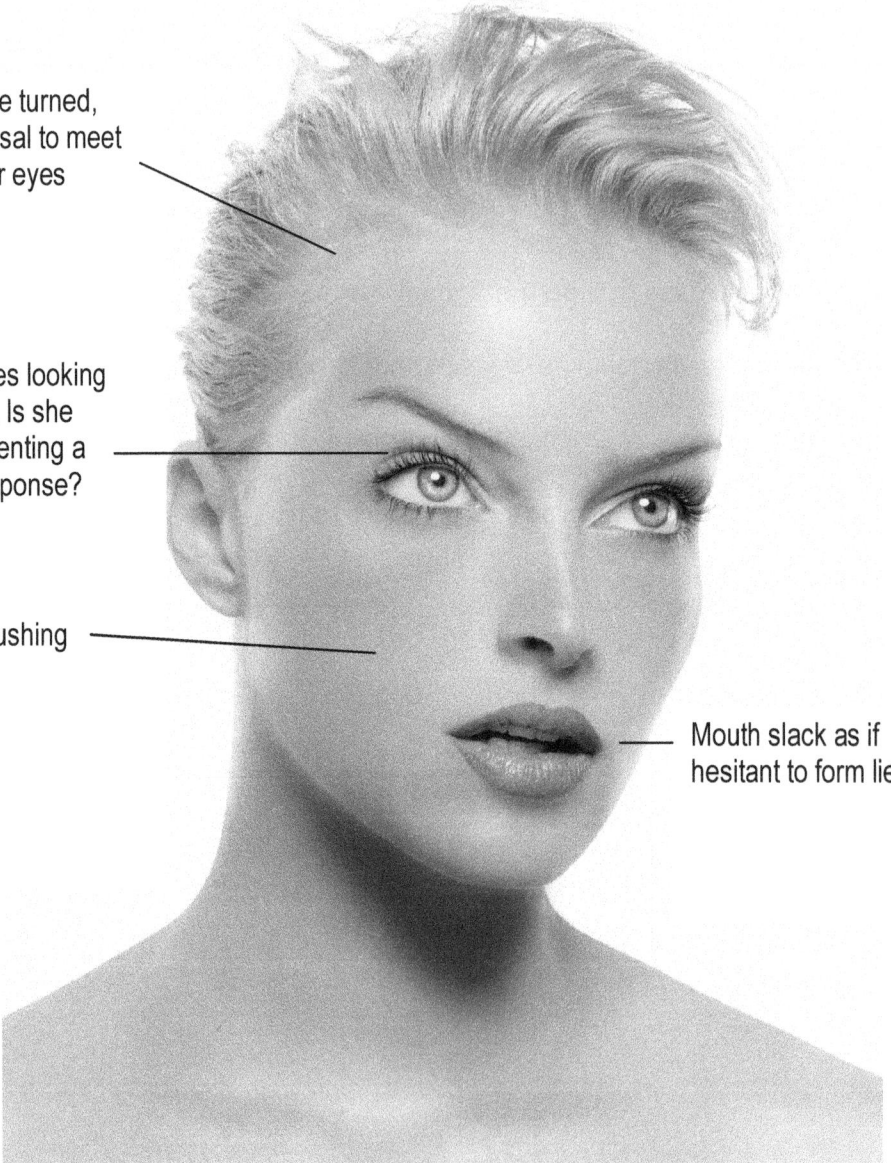

Is It Lie Or Is It Memory?

Actually, eye cues are much more complicated – and fascinating – than the shifty-eyed idea explains.

Separating truth from lies often involves questioning. It's a basic component of police work, courtroom law, military interrogation and much more. As such, a lot of study has gone into reading eye movement to determine if answers given during questioning are truthful or not. This area of study is called Eye Accessing Cues.

The way it works is this. Our brain stores information of various sorts in different areas of our memory. Visual memories, for instance, are stored over in our left brain – the more rational, factual part of our brain. When someone is asked a visual question like "What does it look like?" or "What color was it?" which involves consulting memory, her eyes will actually roll up and to the left (her left side). It's almost like she's trying to look up into her left brain and read the answer stored there.

When that same person is asked something to which she wants to respond with an untruth, she will look up and to the right. Why? Because the right brain is the creative side; she is trying to *create* an answer.

Ah, but be careful. The clues are usually reversed for left-handed people.

Those accessing cues are for visual memory. For auditory answers – "What did the band sound like?" or "What did she say?" – right-handers break right and horizontally for memories, left and sideways for construction – in other words, making an answer up.

If a person is describing something that they have seen or heard, then their eyes should primarily move to visual or auditory *remembered*. Howeve,r if Your Partner is making something up, then his eyes will tend to move to visual or auditory *constructed*, indicating that he is constructing some part of the situation he's describing. This may indicate that Your Partner is either uncertain or untruthful.

The basic eye accessing movements as mapped out by Neurolinguistic Programming co-developers John Grinder and Richard Bandler are:

1. **(VM) Visual Memory:** Eyes up and left.

2. **(VC) Visual Construction:** Eyes up and right.

3. **(AM) Auditory Memory:** Eyes horizontal and to the left.

4. **(AC) Auditory Constructed:** Eyes horizontal and right.

5. **(K) Kinesthetic:** (Accessing something that can be felt – emotionally or physically) Eyes down and right.

6. **(AD) Auditory Digital:** (Talking to him-/herself) Eyes are down and to the left.

For persuasion and questioning purposes, 1-4 are the important cues to remember.

☒ Eye Accessing Cues

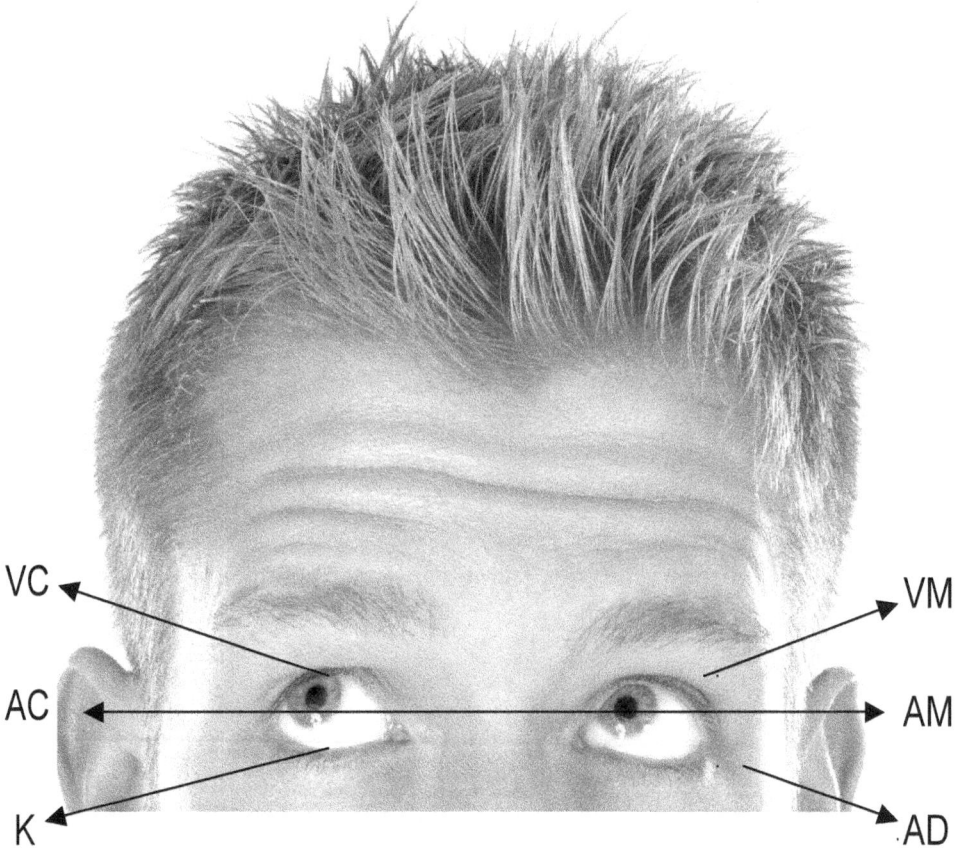

VC   VM

AC   AM

K   AD

NOTE: As universal as these cues are, they are not 100% reliable. Some people have unique responses, some merely focus and refocus without moving their eyes, and some may have a fleeting thought not connected with your question and may be cueing that.

"You boys shouldn't get so excited – it spoils your aim!"

– Wonder Woman

Understanding the inner thoughts and feelings of Your Partner, as reflected in his or her face, gestures and movements, can give you extremely useful insight to use in the persuasion process.

But understanding the body language of Your Persuasion Partner provides just a fraction of the power of this secret.

Remember I said that persuasion was like a well-choreographed dance between you and Your Partner, with you quietly but steadily leading the direction? Knowing their body cues will help you guide them more expertly, but you still have to *guide* them.

So how do you do that?

Well, let's talk about YOUR body language.

In order for you to have the power to persuade, you must first create, what?

Ah. You haven't forgotten the most important secret I have to share, I hope.

TRUST.

TRUST is the power that vitalizes your persuasion super-powers. You will be able to persuade others to the exact limit of how much they TRUST you.

So, your own body language must always speak in a *TRUSTworthy* manner. And it must start doing it *immediately*.

In any personal encounter, your first interaction will often be visual. You will enter the presence of Your Partner or she will approach you. Both of you will register dozens of almost instant-aneous impressions. Dress. Posture. Unique features.

(Just for discussion here we're assuming that you're meeting Your Partner for the first time.) The first impression of *you* will shape his expectations and may set the course for all your interactions.

You know the old saying: "You only have one chance to make a good first impression." It is true; it's crucial for you to make a winning first impression. And by winning, I mean winning TRUST. It is so crucial that it should never be left to chance. A Supersuader never relies on chance – you must be prepared, in control, and ready to quietly and gently take charge of the "dance" from the first second on.

I'm sure you've heard the idea that people form an opinion about others in the first few moments of seeing them. Some experts say the first three minutes are the most important in terms of forming an impression, some say just three seconds. In his fascinating book, *Blink,* Malcolm Gladwell calls the process *thin-*

slicing – the ability of our unconscious to find patterns in situations and behavior based on very narrow slices of experience. Almost instantly.

Whatever the exact timing or mechanism at work, within minutes of meeting someone, we have made hundreds of small observations and drawn dozens of conclusions about his race or nationality, general health and age, energy level, possible occupations, where he might live, and educational and cultural background. We may even have figured his political affiliation and sexual leanings. And since we've practiced this skill every day of our lives, our snap judgments will often be correct.

So, you must act immediately to start projecting TRUST. If you hesitate, the person you're trying to persuade may form a one-second opinion about you that you will have to work doubly hard to change, if you can change it at all. (First impressions often prove to be indelible.)

Luckily, there are things you can do to greatly increase your physical impressiveness and your ability to influence.

The Ugly Truth About Beauty

The truth is, the more attractive you are, the better you'll tend to do in life. Experiment after experiment proves it: the better looking you are, the more people will reward you. It's not fair and it's not right. But it's not incorrect.

Good-looking professors are ranked better teachers by their students, and good-looking students receive significantly higher grades from professors than the average in their class.

If you're an attractive waiter or waitress, you'll get better tips. (You'll do *much* better if you'll also squat down and take the table's orders at eye level.)

A study released by the Federal Reserve Bank of St. Louis states that good-looking people earn about 5% more than average-looking workers. And below-average-looking workers earn 9% less than average.

If you're tall, you'll be assumed more competent and rewarded for it. If your torso is particularly V-shaped, people will attribute all the virile virtues to you. If your bust is large, people will attribute sexual prowess to you.

So, here's an important tip. If you want to truly motivate people and get your way, be beautiful.

But what if your genetics didn't land you in the Lucky Gene Beauty Club? That's okay. We still have a lot of power at our disposal. Rememb   of our minds we're not employing right now? Potential! Now that's *really* beautiful.

Think about what makes someone attractive. **One reason we're drawn to what we call beauty is because it suggests vibrant health, the peak of vitality.** Many of us are tired, bored or lazy; we're naturally drawn to vigor and vibrancy. You just feel better around some vital people, don't you? It's like basking in the warm energy of the sun.

That's the first step you can take to start developing your persuasiveness: develop your vitality, vigor and vibrancy. This is especially true the older you get. The beautiful truth is that you can greatly affect your health and vitality at almost any age.

And you already know how – it's not news.

You know there is a world of resources about getting in shape, losing weight, stopping abuse of substances from cigarettes to drugs. I'm not going to waste time by telling you how important conserving, building, and focusing your health and vitality can be – I'm sure you know it. Your health and vitality affect every part of your life, you know that. And now, you know that it greatly affects your ability to get your own way.

People in general are drawn to healthy people. So, you must either be healthy, vigorous and vital – or **act As If** you are.

The Transforming Secret

Act As If you are. *As If* is the Secret that Transforms; I'll arm you with the power of *As If* in just a few pages. It's going to become a huge component in quickly *supercharging* your persuasion powers.

For now, you'll have to just take this on TRUST:

Whatever age you are, whatever your condition, you should *appear* vital, vibrant and vigorous.

Dress For Persuasion Success

As long as we're on the first visual impression, some basics to remember: Make sure you're well-groomed and well-dressed. By well-dressed I mean dressing about 10% better than Your Persuasion Partner. No more and no less. Your attire should be just slightly more dressy, more expensive, more well-pressed and neat than Your Partner's. It should never dramatically call attention to *you.*

Because, you see, you're not trying to impress Your Partner with how cool or hip or fashion-forward you are. You want to dress to influence, so you must look *TRUST*worthy. And what do people TRUST the most? Their own taste, their own style.

The closer you can present yourself to how Your Partner looks, the quicker you'll begin getting your way.

How do you know how Your Partner dresses when you may be meeting her for the first time? You do research. Recon.

Look her up on the Internet and see if you can find pictures. Ask people who know her. I've been known to stop by the office of a Partner I was planning to meet for the first time and ask for (unneeded) directions from the company receptionist, just to check the general dress code and tone of the office and perhaps get a look at staff photos on display.

Obviously, if you're meeting a Partner of the opposite gender – or someone who wears a special uniform, costume or national dress you're not going to literally dress as they do. The idea is to match them in general formality. Is a bathing suit appropriate in the situation? Is a tuxedo?

You should match them also in general cost and quality of garments (if Your Partner is dressed by Armani and you're dressed by Wal-Mart, you'll have to work harder to build early credibility).

And you should aim for equal stylishness. If he resembles a librarian and you resemble a rock star, there will no doubt be a disconnect between you.

☒ <u>Expert Opinion: The Posture of Persuasion</u>

Julie Steele Blackwood

"Stop slumping," my wife often reminds me. It's more than just a spouse's gripe; it's my personal trainer's orders. Julie Steele Blackwood of BodyShape ProFitness has been shaping competitive athletes and Miss America hopefuls and helping others achieve their fitness

goals for over 20 years. She is certified by the National Federation of Personal Trainers, the American Council on Exercise and Alternate Health and Fitness for Pilates.

How would you like to reduce back problems – the most common physical complaint there is? Okay, if that's not enough, how would you like to also look and feel more confident, charismatic and dynamic? Still not enough? How about adding two inches to your height? And looking 10 pounds lighter. And how about achieving all that in three seconds?

No, it's not some miracle pill or new laser surgery; it's just the everyday good advice your mother probably starting giving you as soon as you could stand: **Stand up straight.**

Fixing flaws in your posture, whatever age, can be one of the fastest self-improvement moves you ever make. It just takes getting into (or back into) the habit of correct posture.

- The spine of the back naturally forms an S-curve

- If hips, shoulders and ears are aligned, your spine's curves should

  also be in line

- Imagine that you are being held up by a string, like a marionette. It goes

  from the top of your head to the ceiling and holds you lightly suspended

- Now try relaxing into the stance while still keeping the string taut. This is

  correct posture

Standing:

- Your shoulders should be back

- Your chest is forward and slightly raised

- Your head should be held upright and straight

- Your stomach should be tucked in, but not tilting the pelvis forward

Sitting:

- Your rear should touch the back of the chair

- Your body weight should rest equally on both hips

- Place a small pillow, or a rolled cloth or towel between your lower back

  and the back of the chair

- Your knees should be at a right angle and a little higher than your hips

- Both feet should be flat on the floor

Neatness Counts – A Lot

As you move closer to Your Partner, it will important that you not present any physical trait that will distract him or make him wonder about you or your upbringing. **Make sure your grooming is also 10% better than Your Partner's.**

- Your teeth should be clean and white and in

  good health

- Your breath should be fresh

- Your skin should be smooth and unblemished

- Your hair should be well-cut in a contemporary

  and flattering manner

- Hair should be clean and appropriately styled

- If you wear facial hair (and many experts say "don't")

  make sure it's neatly trimmed

- Regularly inspect for and remove hairs growing in

  unusual places – in ears, on ears, in noses, on noses, on

  women's chins, on women's lip and so on

- Strong eyebrows can be an impressive and expressive feature of a face. If they're long enough to get tangled or have merged into one, bring in an eyebrow-shaping expert (Men, ask a well-groomed lady whom she recommends)

- Chest hair usually turns more people off than it pleases; display it at your own risk

- And while we're at chest level: A woman's cleavage can be something like nitroglycerine. I certainly wouldn't be foolish enough to say that exposing a hint of femininity – especially a flash of cleavage – cannot be very effective with the right audience, in the right situation. Like nitro, though, its power is badly unpredictable – a little too much and POW. The situation becomes sexual and perhaps not where you wanted it to go. Two bits of classic persuasion advice: Know your audience. Proceed carefully.

- Tatoos: See Chest Hair

• Fingernails should be clean, neat and appropriate. Again, if it fits Your Persuasion Partner's world, wear those air-brushed extensions with inset cubic zirconia. But in most cases, neat-but-not-flashy works best

• Guys, we tend to fall down big-time on the fingernail front. They must be clean at the very least. Not bitten off. Not vampire-length. Clipped relatively short. Better if they're well cared for. Especially if you are trying to influence up-close or across a desk, if you pass documents or point to charts and graphs or use expressive body language, get your fingernails in shape. A periodic manicure is a relatively inexpensive luxury for a man. Try it (But don't be persuaded by the cosmetologist – do not get even clear lacquer on your nails unless you want to appear vain)

Again, your *style* should be as close as possible to Your Prospect's style, if you want to create TRUST. You'll wear your hair differently when you're persuading your way into a

Heavy Metal Revival record deal versus when you're testifying persuasively before Congress, I hope.

Prescription For Persuasiveness

If you do all these things, you will be more physically attractive. That's all good – the more attractive you are, the more naturally persuasive you are – but there are even more powerful changes you can make to boost your influence.

People *are* drawn to physical perfection, we all know that. But even more important, people are especially drawn to *psychological* attractiveness.

Luckily, you don't need to be in some special genetic category containing 12 fashion models and a handful of hunks. Anyone can be psychologically attractive.

There's no question about this. Study after study tells us that everyone feels more comfortable – more TRUSTing – in the presence of someone who seems kindly, friendly and balanced.

Quietly confident. Positive. Strong – in the sense of emotional and physical resources – and secure.

Here's the exact breakdown. People are most attracted to a person who is:

- Genuine

- Kind

- Confident

- Authoritative

Genuine: This has also been described as authentic or *congruent.* I know this is a lot coming at you fast, but all of this will become clear and sensible to you soon.

People also appreciate a person who is kind. Other descriptions include loving, caring and non-judgmental.

People tend to TRUST others with unshakeable TRUST in themselves – confidence.

And, if you seem to have authority, it is easier for people to *intellectually* justify their TRUST in you.

All Objects Seek Balance

Many people's lives are out of balance. They feel confused, overworked and overwhelmed. No matter how important any of us may be, or how successful, or how seemingly strong, deep inside most of us are unsure. A lot of us are anxious. Some are flat-out terrified.

One of the wryest, and truest, comments I heard in my years in the ad agency business was uttered by a young account executive at the end of a grueling day: "I think I'll call in scared tomorrow."

And all around most of us are other people with problems – some with severe problems – and people who want things from us, who are downers, who are nay-sayers, who threaten to siphon the spirit out of us like one of Harry Potter's Dementors.

When we first meet people, we often go on Orange Alert – to protect us in case the other person is out to take something from us. Or infect us with their problems. Perhaps even hurt us in some way. In case they're out to unbalance our lives even more.

We steel ourselves, we arm ourselves mentally and emotionally.

We also show that wariness or disTRUST in our posture, our expression, our breathing, our entire physical presence – **our bodies always reflect what is going on in our minds.** And that's what makes the insights you will learn in this book possible and powerful.

On the other hand, aren't we almost magnetically drawn to others who seem more balanced than we are, who seem physically and emotionally healthy, who are apparently without major problems? It feels good to be around people like that; they don't sap our energy, they have their own inner resources. They're not needy. (In fact, maybe we can even draw some psychic energy from them.)

What a relief! No need for arming ourselves. No need for protective walls.

Have you ever heard the phrase, "She has a disarming smile" or "He's disarming in his honesty"?

Starting with the first image Your Partner has of you, you can be *disarming*. Before you even open your mouth, you can start building TRUST by radiating the image of a completely likeable person – upbeat, confident, way too nice to ever hard sell.

When there is nothing to resist, Your Partner relaxes. He opens up; he is *disarmed* of resistance.

"Wait a minute," some of you may be thinking. *"I'm not that balanced. I'm not that confident. In fact, I'm confused, too, a lot of them time. I have plenty of problems – and I do want something from this person, I want them to give me my way!"*

Remember the Transforming Secret, As If?

Many superheroes have a Transforming Secret, a special word or action or *something* that causes them to transform from their imperfect ordinary self into a superpowerful being. Young Billy Batson uttered the mystic word Shazam and transformed into an adult Captain Marvel. The crippled Dr. Donald Blake tapped his staff on the ground and became the mythological Mighty Thor. You will have As If.

You will act As If you already are a Supersuader. You will imitate the persona of a Supersuader hero, that will be the source of your Supersuader Identity: Genuine, caring, supremely confident but never conceited, with quiet authority.

In other words, *superTRUSTworthy*.

Now, some of you are probably saying, "As If? You mean we're going to be faking genuineness?"

Well, yes, that's what I'm suggesting.

Fake It Till You Make It

Alcoholics Anonymous – an organization as experienced in real-life human behavior as any I know – gives this advice: "Fake it till you make it." It's a very powerful concept; ask any developmental psychologist. By mimicking behaviors, we train our brain how to make them our own. As infants and children, a major component of our development comes from observing our parents and others around us as they speak, gesture, use facial expressions, walk and so on. We try to imitate them, probably fail some, and then eventually we master the behavior. By using others as models, we learn to pull up, stand, toddle, walk and finally run – and the once-mimicked behaviors become a permanent part of who we are.

This fact leads us to the full Transformational Secret – the second most important secret you will learn from this book:

You can become *whatever you want to become* if you:

• **Imagine it vividly enough**

• **Act As If consistently**

• **Allow it to become true**

I know that sounds just too good to be real. One of the most important lessons in life – how to be the person of your dreams – can't be that simple, can it?

Try it for yourself.

Smile at everyone and everything for 60 minutes; I bet you'll feel more upbeat and positive at the end of the hour. If you're still not convinced, then frown at everyone for an hour; see if you don't feel fittingly miserable.

Once you learn more about the actual psychological and physical (and physiological) aspects of persuasion, you'll see that what we're talking about doing here is using essentially the same tactics you'll employ in convincing Your Partners. You're just turning the techniques on yourself first.

In fact, this is so important that it gives rise to Blackwood's First Law of Persuasion: **You must be persuaded first.**

The Origins Of Supersuader

Now, maybe you're thinking, *"I can't act. I didn't even get cast in the grade school play!"* TRUST me, you don't need to act. You just need to imitate.

Everyone can imitate, we've been doing it all our lives. As we said, when you were an infant, you imitated the way your parents stood up and walked. In school, you imitated how popular kids did things, how they talked, how *they* stood and walked, the attitude, the look. And, in our immaturity, some of us aped the unpopular kids with devastating accuracy.

Here's all you have to do: Find someone to imitate. When you say the word TRUST who jumps into your mind? A movie icon like Gary Cooper or Tom Hanks? Your grandmother? The campus star when you were in college?

Remember what the majority of people say they expect in a person they TRUST:

- Genuineness (authenticity or congruence – "being yourself")

- Love or caring (being a kind person, a fair person)

- Confidence (being balanced, positive)

- Authority (wisdom, expertise)

Who do you know that is a model of those characteristics? Close your eyes and picture that person as vividly as you can in your mind.

After a moment, try taking on the characteristics you admire in that person. Let the essence of that person affect the way you stand, your expression, your energy level.

It's really not that difficult. Monkeys do it. I know you can, too.

It will be easiest to accomplish, of course, if you can find a model who is already somewhat like you. The more you can make needed refinements in your identity, as opposed to serious changes, the quicker you can get your persona up and persuasive.

There is no reason at all why you can't take on the TRUST characteristics of someone of the opposite sex. You just need to make sure you're copying the TRUSTworthy *character*, not the male or female expression of it. (Mimicking stereotypes of the opposite sex is never recommended as a reliable TRUST-builder.)

Once you've got the look, posture, energy and gestures, try going deeper into the character. What kind of "vibe" does this person give off when you first see him or her? How does she show her kindness? How does he demonstrate his positive attitude?

Then you refine it further and personalize it. Ask yourself: "If I were really full of easy-going confidence, how would *I* stand? How would I walk?"

If your were an authority, how would you most likely sound? How much would you speak?

Try out small components of your Supersuader Identity in situations where you have nothing to lose if you're not quite convincing – with the store clerk when you're buying something, for instance, or with new people you meet in social situations. Try assuming an attitude that says, "I'm a caring person" or "My opinion is valuable; I'm an expert." See how they react to you, see how *you* react to *them* when you're projecting this persuasion persona. (It's a two-way interaction, remember.)

Consistently practice the persona and keep refining it. I promise that if you do, one day you will realize that it now fits you as naturally and comfortably as your favorite pair of jeans.

Until then, what? Fake it till you make it.

Superheroes always wear a disguise, don't they?

If Your Partner Knows You…

Obviously, much of the preceding information concerns the first face-to-face meeting with Your Partner. What if Your Partner already knows you?

Then the same strategy applies, it must just be handled more slowly and delicately. Obviously, the closer Your Partner is to you emotionally – family, spouse, best friend – and the more experience he has with you, the faster he will notice any abrupt change in your behavior or attitude. He'll need to watch you change over a certain period of time to believe you are genuine (the first and most crucial component of TRUST).

But you really shouldn't have to drag it out very long. Modern man is very dynamic; we make sweeping changes all the time – starting instant relationships, suddenly ending long-term ones; quitting and getting new jobs, careers, homes, hometowns, families, bodies, you name it.

Chances are you have reserves of TRUST already stockpiled in the hearts and minds of people who know you the best. You'll just need to strengthen it over two or three interactions.

Warning: Don't try to convince your family or close friends that you're an authority if you're really not. You probably shouldn't bother trying to convince them even if you really are.

☒

There are other ways of first communicating with Persuasion Partners – via telephone or other broadcast devices such as radio or television, or else via writing as with letters, emails, books, pamphlets, articles, etc.

I plan to cover those important topics in later Persuasion Superpower guides – this is a book about reading body language cues (and projecting the most persuasive body language yourself). I will pause here though for a short sidebar on developing your most persuasive voice by a noted expert on that subject. Voice tone, pitch, accent and rate of speech are all paralinguistic cues and are worthy of study as part of non-verbal communication.

☒ <u>Expert Opinion: Pitch-Perfect Voice</u>
Helen Wilkie

If there is one quality that, more than any other, moves listeners to be persuaded by our arguments, it is confidence. When someone appears confident in his or her own statements, those listening are more likely to assume they are correct. It's possible to dissect this appearance of self-confidence so that we can develop it for ourselves.

Think of someone in your organization who exudes self-confidence, and whose views everyone instinctively assumes are correct. Close your eyes and try to "hear" that person deliver a statement, perhaps at a meeting. Where is the pitch of the voice? How quickly does the person speak? Generally speaking, a low register and slightly slower than average speed give authority to a speaker's words. At the opposite end of the scale, someone who speaks quickly, in a high-pitched, squeaky voice, generally has little credibility.

You can work on lowering the pitch of your voice if you feel it is a little too close to the "squeaky" end of the scale. Here's an exercise that helps. Choose a tune you know well, and simply hum it out loud. The well-known tune of "Happy Birthday" works well for this, due to its predominantly mid-range notes. The register of your humming is your natural voice pitch. Now gradually slide out of the humming and say a few words on the same level as the humming. Next, hum the tune again, but this time consciously at a lower pitch, then slide out into the words again. Do this several times, as long as the spoken word is comfortable.

Practice until you can lower your pitch at will, and consciously use the new level as often as possible at work.

Speech that is too fast is also a credibility robber, but fortunately this is easy to correct. Listen to your own voice on tape, and if it sounds too fast, simply slow down.

Here's an effective method of improving your overall delivery.

Choose someone on television who has credibility, in whose words you feel inclined to place your TRUST– perhaps a newscaster or interviewer. Audiotape a five-minute segment of that person's speech, then listen to it several times. Now listen to the first minute and repeat it yourself, emulating the speaker's tone as much as possible – that means the speed, pitch and intonation. Do the same with each minute in turn, and then try the whole segment. This technique is called "tape and ape" and it will go a long way to improving your own delivery. These people are professionals whose jobs depend on how well they present information—doesn't that also, in a way, describe you?

Helen Wilkie is a professional speaker, consultant and author who helps companies do better business through better communication. Her latest book is *The Hidden Profit Center*. To received free monthly tips and techniques on communication, visit http://www.mhwcom.com or http://www.HiddenProfitCenter.com and sign up for "Communi-keys." Reach Helen Wilkie at 416-966-5023 or hwilkie@mhwcom.com.

Your Entrance

If you have to enter an open door, walk right in without hesitation. If a door is closed, knock once or twice firmly and then smoothly open the door and walk in. Isn't that how a confident person would enter?

Don't get excited. Move slowly. Slow movements are very practical – they make you appear calm and self-assured while actually helping hold down any nervous clumsiness that might shatter that image.

Note: The higher on the social scale you are – or desire to be – the less you should gesture and the smaller and more controlled your gestures should be. It's as if the hidden message is that people with status don't *have* to move.

Warning: People from more emotive cultures and upbringing may think small, controlled gestures show a lack of conviction or even truthfulness. In most situations, lead with smaller gestures and then become more expansive if you see that Your Partner uses larger gestures.

Exhibit balance and command as you cross a room, holding eye contact with the most powerful or senior person in the room.

Now you're entering into Your Partner's *personal space* and the rules of proximics kick in.

Proximics is the science of personal space and how we use it and react to it. This subject is so crucial in interpersonal conduct that you probably already know most of this by practice or instinct. Even more than imitation, you've been practicing this with every person you have ever met – for most of your life.

The normal interaction area of most humans is between four feet and a foot and a half. There can't be much involvement with anyone farther away than 48 inches; closer than 18 inches and you have entered the intimate space of someone – and that may make her irritated, alarmed or outright hostile.

Not a good way to build TRUST.

It's not an exact science. People have different spaces they prefer and again it can vary by culture and upbringing.

Probably the most effective position is about two to three feet away from Your Partner. Your objective is to be as close as possible without violating Your Partner's personal space.

(Now is when those grooming reminders I gave you will pay off.)

Then you ease in smoothly and slowly throughout the interaction. Do not make a move closer than 18 or 19 inches unless it is with specific intention – to shake hands or perhaps exchange papers.

In general, it pays to work farther back with a new partner, closer in with a familiar one. Men can work a bit closer in with women – if they're careful to act TRUSTworthy. Women may want to work a little farther back with men.

Start closer to those near your age, farther back for a partner much older or younger. That brings us to Blackwood's Proximity Prescription: **The more you're like your prospect – in**

age, look, background and status – the closer in you'll

probably be able to start. (Remember, the more Your Partner

sees herself in you, the faster you'll establish persuasive bonds

of TRUST.)

Whatever the proximic situation, there is often one

incongruously intimate moment in meetings, even between total

strangers – sometimes between sworn enemies: a clasping and

holding and squeezing of hands. It does sound pretty intimate

when you describe a handshake like that, doesn't it?

The Perfect Handshake

The handshake started as something quite practical, a way

of showing that you weren't approaching with a weapon in your

hand. In other words, you could be *TRUSTed*.

Today, it's an almost universal ritual, and should be dealt

with decisively and without fuss. Your hands should be warm and

dry, of course. If they're wet and clammy, carry a handkerchief

and give them a vigorous drying just before you approach Your

Partner – but *never* where they can see. (You're radiating assurance and balance, remember?)

So, handshakes: warm and dry hands. Grip firm but never vice-like. Hand to hand, interlocking palms, web of thumb to web of thumb; no finger shakes. No pumping the hand up and down. A steady squeeze, hold the grip for a count of two or three.

TIP: Once your confidence increases, try pulling the prospect toward you just a bit as you shake. It reinforces your lack of fear (confidence) and your outgoing warmth (caring).

But do not get so warm that you try the two-handed handclasp favored by politicians and drunks. It's overwhelming at best and overbearing at worst. To some, it suggests that you're trying to dominate them.

In the right circumstances, the two-handed handshake favored by former President Bill Clinton – right hand shaking yours, left hand warmly grasping your shoulder or arm – can make you feel like you're the only person he came there to see. But I can't pull it off successfully, and you probably can't either.

The handshake is a touchy moment, literally and figuratively. You've moved inside someone's circle of intimate space. You are gripping their (probably) dominant hand and holding it immobile.

Get in, get out.

Back off to a safe distance. That is, one that feels safe for Your Partner. Your mission now is to slowly, *gently*, unthreateningly move in closer and closer throughout your entire interaction.

Handing or showing something to Your Partner will allow you to get a momentary pass inside her intimate space. Usually, when you step back, you'll be able position yourself closer to Your Partner than before without alarming her.

Each time you move in close, and then retreat away without unpleasant incident, you are showing Your Partner that you mean no harm and are a friendly, good-natured person. You are training her to TRUST you.

Surely you've approached a dog you didn't know. The best way, of course, is to ease in slowly, making sure at each step that the animal doesn't react with fear or dominance before moving closer. This tactic, applied with honest kindness and goodwill, will usually have all but the most wary dogs eating out of your hand within a few minutes.

It works with people, too.

Sit!

Jockeying for favored status within groups has trained humans and other primates in a potent form of body language – social or status positioning. You're human, you know how it works. The Head Honcho/Alpha Male/Father Figure sits at the head of the table, in the biggest chair, or in the spot with the best view. The Alpha Female or Beta Male takes the Mother Figure position opposite him at the foot of the table or in the second-best spot. When seated, equals tend to face each other, so often do enemies. Intimates often sit, how? See, you know: side by side.

When you notice people in a side-by-side position, looking off in the same direction, it's a pretty good sign they're totally harmonious – as if they're sharing the same view or vision of the world.

If they're turned more toward each other, you may surmise that they're close friends or relatives. If they're turned away from each other, willfully ignoring the person who is right next to them, you may guess that their views do *not* match. Or they're relatives.

So, thinking about all that, how would you position yourself for maximum persuasiveness in a one-to-one interaction?

If you're standing, you should aim for a face-to-face position, turned perhaps 10 degrees to your left to reduce any suggestion of aggressiveness or confrontation. It's a simple position to assume from a handshake. It's handshake, step back right, step back at a 10% angle with the left. There you are.

Then throughout the exchange, as you move in closer, also slowly open up the angle between you until (this may take several exchanges) you reach side by side. The body language message Your Partner's subconscious registers is that you two are literally on the same side. Then you really *are* partners.

If it looks as if you've moved too close, too fast, just quietly ease back. As you interact (and distract), begin to move in again gently.

Be very clear in your intent – in your own mind and in Your Partner's mind. The only reason you keep moving closer to Your Partner is because the two of you are feeling more and more comfortable together, drawn together like old friends chatting beside a crackling fireplace on an October evening.

If you're sitting, try to get on the same side of the table as Your Partner, at least for a few moments to point something out in a document or place something on the table for inspection.

If Your Partner places you in the classic "business meeting" situation – he on one side of a desk, you on the other – and keeps a table between you as a barrier, do your best to move your chair at least to the open *side* of the desk.

This can be effective in someone else's office; I often move the guest chair a little to the side as I approach the desk, as if to make room. When I sit, I "accidentally" shift it a little more, and so on.

When it's most effective, though, is when it's *your* desk. Coming out from behind the protection of your furniture and meeting Your Partner in more open surroundings instantly signals your confidence and your intention to be friendly and open. That's a lot you can accomplish just by moving to a different chair.

If you do your persuading in your office, try putting two guest chairs squarely facing your desk. When I was an advertising creative director, I always set up my office that way. Agency creative directors tend to have to console and reassure a lot of people – clients who want to bail on a concept before it gets a chance to work, account service folk who are afraid the creative will lose the business, and creative types who feel that the other two are essentially empty suits.

Whenever I had one of those meetings, I'd start by stepping out from behind my desk and sitting next to my visitor, both of us facing the same way. It helps.

"It's Rude To Point"

Your mother probably told you not to point your finger at other people because it is bad manners. I'm telling you not to point at people because it is bad body language.

Pointing your finger is aggressive and is often seen as hostile. It can be like a symbolic stab or a mimed shooting. The pointing finger is associated with guilt and exposure. ("Is that man in the courtroom? Point to him now.")

Even when we have nothing to feel guilty about, the pointing finger can make us uncomfortable, even angry. So, common sense says, "It's dumb to point."

You will be called upon from time to time to indicate a person from some distance away or make a strong point that you want to emphasize with a dynamic gesture. How can you do that and still display positive body signals?

Watch seasoned speakers, especially politicians. They use several pointing substitutes that allow them to do all that. The three most common are practical and elegant.

First is the lightly closed hand with the thumb slightly extended and resting on the curled index finger. It's almost as if you're holding an invisible pointer. Picture former President Clinton speaking; he uses that gesture constantly for emphasis. It's so recognizable that in gesture researcher Adam Kendon's listing of all "quotable gestures" – hand motions that have recognizable meaning throughout a culture – ninth on the list is Clinton Thumb. It really might better be called Kennedy Thumb, as Clinton no doubt borrowed it consciously or unconsciously from his hero, J.F.K. – a master persuader.

The next gesture is similar except the index and second finger uncurl a little more from the rest and the thumb tip touches their tips, almost like the position for snapping your fingers, or as if you're holding up an invisible coin.

A third variation is essentially the gesture we all know as signaling "OK" – the circle made by touching thumb and index finger, the other fingers opened out in widening arcs. When turned with the palm mostly downward, it can be used for a pointing gesture or an emphatic gesture (like sticking a pin in something). Turned with the palm sideways, it becomes almost a musical conductor's gesture, and is useful for showing that you're making measured, reasonable points. Turned with the palm up or out, it becomes emotional, a plea for understanding – even spiritual.

The turned-out gesture is used in many depictions of Buddha. It is know as Vitarka Mudra, the mudra or gesture that indicates intellectual discussion, debate or appeasement.

8th Century Chinese Buddha, showing Vitarka Mudra

Deep Inner-Mind Persuasion

So far in this book, we've explored two crucial persuasion skills:

1. Reading what Your Partner is thinking

2. Projecting your most persuasive persona

There is a third, even more powerful way in which you can use body language to change a person's mind to your way of thinking. Now we'll learn about:

3. Changing Your Partner's feelings

I hope by now you are starting to understand the connection between what is thought in the mind and what is shown physically, via the combination of gestures, postures, movements, expressions and non-verbal sounds commonly referred to as body language.

A little more complicated to understand, perhaps, but even more important is the idea that by mimicking behaviors, we learn to "own" them. Practice not only makes perfect, it makes personality.

Now, we'll combine those two insights – and everything else you've learned in this guide – and focus them like a persuasion-ray onto Your Partner. This is where your Supersuader identity discovers its true power, so please follow closely.

You know that by imitating certain gestures, postures and behaviors, you can actually change the way you feel. If you smile, you'll gradually start to feel happier; if you frown, you'll start to feel unhappy. So, it's obvious that our body language not only *reflects* what we are feeling and thinking, it can actually work in reverse just as easily – it can *transform* how we feel and think. **And it can transform how Your Partner feels and thinks, deep at an unconscious level.**

Here's where the real persuasion dance begins, with you leading. But first, you must synchronize with Your Partner.

Mirroring

If you make a careful study of human interaction, you'll notice that as people become in sync with each other, they begin to use the same gestures, they assume similar postures and expressions – in close rapport, even breathing patterns may be similar.

If you *cause* that process to happen, if you consciously and subtly echo back to a Partner her own body language, she will almost immediately begin to feel more rapport with you.

Mirroring is one way to do that. As if you were looking in a mirror; you take a reversed version of Your Partner's stance or position, you reflect back her gestures on the opposite side. You do it slowly, three to five seconds after she makes a move.

She leans to the right in her chair; after three to five seconds, you lean to your left. She crosses her legs left over right; after a few seconds, you cross your legs right over left.

Never do it quickly, never do it overtly, move slowly and easily and several seconds after she does. Otherwise, you risk looking like you're "aping" or mocking her. Mockery is an insult, imitation is the sincerest form of flattery, remember?

It's so simple, yet it's packed with awesome power that affects both you and Your Partner.

On his side, if you keep it subtle enough to bypass his critical eye and sink directly into his unconscious, he will just start feeling in tune with you.

And you should feel that, too. By imitating Your Partner's body language, you should be more easily able to "get into his head," as we used to say in the 70s. Actually, *you are climbing into his **body**, and starting to feel some of what **he's feeling**.*

Mirroring, naturally, works best in a face-to-face position.

Matching

Matching is simply mimicking Your Partner's posture, moves and expressions on the same side. If he scratches his left ear, four seconds later you scratch your left ear. If he turns slightly to the right when he's talking to you, you pause and then turn slightly to your right.

This can work in anything from a face-to-face to a side-by-side orientation.

Pacing

Once you get your body in sync with Your Partner's, take it down to an even deeper level by replicating his pacing. Does he act quickly? Talk slowly? Take on that pacing yourself.

One of the most effective ways to use this form of rapport building is to match Your Partner's breathing. Does she take deep breaths or shallow ones, quick breaths or long, slow ones? Again, don't make it obvious, but slowly start to breath that way yourself.

Within seconds, the bond between you and Your Partner will be stronger – almost primal. From this point on, your *feel* for this person should grow richer and deeper, almost as if you're channeling his personality somehow. You are – you're channeling his physical being and physiology.

Leading

You may be saying to yourself, *I thought I was supposed to be the leader of this process, all this sounds like following.*

Mirroring or matching and pacing are necessary to get you and Your Partner super-synched, so to speak. Only then will you have created the rapport required for you to begin to lead.

After you have successfully mirrored or matched Your Partner for a while and your interaction has become warmer and more natural (maybe even primal), you should *shift some aspect of your position.* Put a hand on a hip, or shift your weight to the other foot, or cock your head slightly to one side. If Your Partner follows *your* lead now, you have rapport and are beginning to gain **influence.**

If Your Partner doesn't echo your move, just go back to echoing her for a bit and try leading again in a few minutes.

NOTE: One of the most amazing things about the skills in this guide is how incredibly easy and natural they are. They mostly stem from behaviors we've already been practicing for years. Leading through body language is not something most of us are experienced with, though, so it may need a bit more practice.

Don't feel bad if you don't succeed the first time you try this. Various Partners will have different degrees of sensitivity to this tactic – some may be more resistant, others more susceptible.

This certainly isn't the only key to persuasion, though it's a powerful one. Just gently keep trying – and remember not to show your frustration through your face or body.

Relax; it always happens more easily when you aren't trying.

(And remember not to look shocked or to giggle when it does happen!)

Once you find that Your Partner is following your lead, you can begin to reprogram his or her feelings.

Changing Your Partner's Feelings

Throughout your interaction, watch for the signs of resistance and negativity you've learned about in this guide. When you see negative body language forming – crossed arms for instance – mirror or match the behavior a few seconds later.

Probe verbally (gently) for the source of the resistance. Explain your case (request, idea, etc.) again, stressing the best "selling" points. As you do so, slowly lead Your Partner into a more open and positive posture. Try to lead her into a relaxing sigh or deep breath. Relax yourself, of course, and let a deep positive feeling flow through you.

You will find that with enough gentle leading, you can move many Partners to a more open posture, and a more open mind. Because Your Partner's inner mind – literal and quick to judge as all our inner minds are – says to itself, *"Hey, I'm relaxed. I must feel good about what this nice person is saying."*

Persuaded?

Earlier in this guide, I made the statement that you can become pretty much whatever you desire to be if you:

- **Imagine it vividly enough**

- **Act As If consistently**

- **Allow it to become true**

We've explored the first two bullets. The last is the final advice I want to leave with you. *And it's as important as anything you've learned in this book, so please consider this:*

For a variety of reasons, some of us do not accept positive change in ourselves. Perhaps deep down, some of us don't truly believe we deserve to succeed – some guilt or perceived flaw holds us back. Perhaps we are overly sensitive to failing, so we refrain from trying to better ourselves. Perhaps we're just lazy or tired and we don't want to put forth the effort to change.

For whatever reason, some of us consistently deny ourselves the ability to grow and improve.

Remember the First Law of Persuasion: **You must be persuaded first?**

If you cannot do this because you're held back by your own inner mind, you will be forever hampered in your ability to persuade others dynamically.

The good news is you probably don't need years of intensive psychoanalysis or other therapy to get rid of many of these self-imposed limitations. Remember how literal your inner mind can be? You just need to change your mind using classic persuasion techniques.

Start by coming up with a simple, positive affirmation that you can "teach" your inner mind. Here are a few examples:

"I give myself permission to succeed beyond my wildest dreams."

"I allow myself to be whatever I want to be, now and forever."

"I am a Supersuader, and nothing can stop me."

Once you've found an affirmation that feels natural, try adding the most persuasively positive of all words: **"Yes!"**

"I succeed because I have persuasion power. Yes!"

Adding "Yes!" brings an even deeper level of acceptance to the statement. Practice saying your affirmation in the morning, when you awaken and before the demands of the day press in on you. Repeat it at the end of the day, as you drift off to sleep.

At the edge of sleep is what is called "twilight sleep" – that half-asleep, half-awake state we all know. Those of you who believe you cannot be hypnotized, and never have been, may be surprised to know that "twilight sleep" is just another term for a trance state. You are in a hypnotic trance at those times (and many other times – ever "zoned out" while you were driving?).

So, those naturally hypnotic states offer a perfect opportunity for persuading your already-open mind. But, you can get use out of your affirmation at any time.

Soon, you may find that you can elicit a positive, persuasive state just by repeating to yourself: "Yes!"

I know that if you allow yourself to use the skills I have taught you in X-Ray Body Reading, you will be well on your way to getting your way.

I know you can do it!

Yes!

Resources

Many books, articles, television programs and other forms of information have shaped the knowledge in X-Ray Body Reading. Here are some of the most useful in furthering your powers:

Body Language
Fast, Julius
New York: M. Evans, 2002

Winning Moves: The Body Language of Selling
Delmar, Ken
New York: Warner Books, 1984

Body Language
Wainwright, Gordon R.
Chicago: Contemporary Pub., 2003

The Definitive Book of Body Language
Pease, Allan
New York: Bantam Books, 2006

Body Language
Quilliam, Susan
Buffalo, NY: Firefly Books, 2004

Power Persuasion
Barron, David R. and Kaus, Danek S.
Bandon, OR: Robert D. Reed Publishers, 2005

The Hypnotic Salesman
Eason, Adam
Eagan, MN: Network 3000 Publishing, 2007

Blink: The Power of Thinking Without Thinking
Gladwell, Malcolm
New York: Little, Brown, 2005

Never Be Lied To Again
Lieberman, David J., PhD.
New York: St. Martin's Griffin, 1998